LET'S ROCK!

WHAT ARE METAMORPHIC ROCKS?

Molly Aloian

Crabtree Publishing Company

www.crabtreebooks.com

Author: Molly Aloian
Editor-in-Chief: Paul Challen
Project coordinator: Kathy Middleton
Photo research: Melissa McClellan
Designer: Tibor Choleva
Proofreaders: Rachel Stuckey, Crystal Sikkens
Production coordinator: Amy Salter
Production: Kim Richardson
Prepress technician: Amy Salter

Consultant: Kelsey McCormack, B.Sc, M.Sc, PhD
McMaster University

Title page: White marble quarry in Marina di Carrara, Italy

Special Thanks: Stu Harding, Lucyna Bethune,
Sandor Monos and Sandee Ewasiuk

This book was produced for Crabtree Publishing
Company by Silver Dot Publishing.

Illustrations:
© David Brock: page 7

Photographs and reproductions:
© Dreamstime.com: title page (Leon1) and pages 4 (Juliengrondin),
6/7 large (Juliengrondin), 8 right (Gyeah), 10/11 large (Vasiu), 12 top
(Moonmeister), 13 (Aardlumens), 14/15 large (Bridgetjones), 17 middle
(Chris Crowley), 17 middle (Marek Uliasz), 18 (Alehnia), 24/25 large
(Gaja), 26 top (Kitano), 27 bottom (Elifranssens)

© istockphoto.com: headline image (trumpetmonkey), pages 6 top (Dmitry
Demidovich), 7 large (lissart), 12 middle (vora), 12 bottom (seraficus), 15
bottom (only_fabrizio), 17 top (lubilub), 17 middle (Barcin), 17 bottom
(dmitriyd), 21 left (efesan), 21 right (efesan), 22 bottom (fotoVoyager),
22/23 large (miralex), 22 top (KeeTron), 25 left (Takis_Milonas), 25 right
(lissart), 26/27 large (RoyalFive), 29 top (PenelopeB), 29 middle (cfarish)

© Shutterstock.com: background image (sevda) pages 4/5 large (Roca),
5 top (paul prescott), 5 bottom(Walter G Arce), 6 bottom (marekuliasz),
8/9 large (Pichugin Dmitry), 8 left (Andrea Danti), 12/13 large (Kevin H
Knuth), 14 (Tom Grundy), 15 top (JR Trice), middle (Sue Smith), 16 (Adrian
Zenz), 18/19 large (Wendy Kaveney Photography), 19 top (Dirk Ott), 19
bottom (Hallgerd), 20/21 large (Stephen Bonk), 20 (Joe Goodson), 21 top
(Marafona), 22 left (minik), 23 top (AridOcean), 23 bottom (CLM), 24
bottom (Joe West), 24 top (sspopov), 26 left (Bork), 27 top (Jeff R. Clow),
27 middle (MBWTE Photos), 28 left (Yarchyk), 29 bottom (Hanka B.)

© Callan Bentley: page 11

Tectonic Map courtesy of the U.S. Geological Survey: pages 9, 15 top right

Library and Archives Canada Cataloguing in Publication

Aloian, Molly
     What are metamorphic rocks? / Molly Aloian.

(Let's rock)
Includes index.
Issued also in an electronic format.
ISBN 978-0-7787-7229-3 (bound).--ISBN 978-0-7787-7234-7 (pbk.)

     1. Rocks, Metamorphic--Juvenile literature. I. Title. II. Series:
Let's rock (St. Catharines, Ont.)

QE475.A2A46 2011   j552'.4   C2010-904130-5

Library of Congress Cataloging-in-Publication Data

Aloian, Molly.
  What are metamorphic rocks? / Molly Aloian.
     p. cm. -- (Let's rock)
  Includes index.
   ISBN 978-0-7787-7229-3 (reinforced lib. bdg. : alk. paper) -- ISBN 978-
0-7787-7234-7 (pbk. : alk. paper) -- ISBN 978-1-4271-9523-4 (electronic
(PDF)
  1. Rocks, Metamorphic--Juvenile literature. I. Title. II. Series.

   QE475.A2A46 2011
   552'.4--dc22

                                                           2010024597

Crabtree Publishing Company

www.crabtreebooks.com   1-800-387-7650

Printed in the U.S.A./082010/BA20100709

Published in Canada
Crabtree Publishing
616 Welland Ave.
St. Catharines, Ontario
L2M 5V6

Published in the United States
Crabtree Publishing
PMB 59051
350 Fifth Avenue, 59ᵗʰ Floor
New York, New York 10118

Published in the United Kingdom
Crabtree Publishing
Maritime House
Basin Road North, Hove
BN41 1WR

Published in Australia
Crabtree Publishing
386 Mt. Alexander Rd.
Ascot Vale (Melbourne)
VIC 3032

CONTENTS

WHERE DID IT ALL BEGIN?

You may have noticed that there are different types of rocks on Earth. Each type is created in a different way. Metamorphic rocks are one type of rock. There are metamorphic rocks all over the world. The word "metamorphic" means "change of form" in Greek. Over time, different types of rocks change form to become metamorphic rocks.

HOT, HOT, HOT!

Certain conditions on Earth cause some rocks to become metamorphic rocks. Intense heat can create metamorphic rocks. The temperature deep inside Earth is very hot—so hot that some rock melts and becomes thick **magma**. Heat from magma can cause other kinds of rock to change into metamorphic rock. For example, the heat from magma can cause limestone to change into marble. Marble is a metamorphic rock.

▶ Magma that reaches Earth's surface during a volcanic eruption is known as lava.

HOT STUFF

✴ Most rock melts at temperatures between 392°F (200°C) and 2,012°F (1,100°C).

ROCKY EARTH

✴ Sedimentary rocks and igneous rocks are two other types of rocks found on Earth. Sedimentary rocks are made from **sediment**. Igneous rocks are made from magma and lava.

TYPES OF METAMORPHISM

There are different types of metamorphism. Heat from magma can cause contact metamorphism. Intense heat from **lava** bakes the layers of rock surrounding it.

A change in great quantities of rock over a large area is called regional metamorphism.

▼ *In an oven, heat changes pizza dough into crust, just like the heat from magma can change limestone into marble.*

◄ *The Himalayas mountain range was formed by forces of regional metamorphism.*

SHOCKING!

Shock metamorphism occurs when asteroids or comets collide with Earth's surface, producing powerful shock waves that cause rocks to change form underground.

◄ *Meteorite craters often contain rocks changed by the pressure of the meteor's impact.*

MAKING CONTACT

Contact metamorphism happens when heat from magma that is close by causes new **minerals** to form in rocks. Minerals are chemicals that occur naturally on Earth in the form of crystals. Salt and calcium are two kinds of minerals.

BAKED ROCK

Contact metamorphism often takes place in rocks that are next to the spot where magma enters Earth's crust, known as an **intrusion**. A large igneous intrusion is called a **batholith**. The closer rocks are to the batholith, the more they will be altered by heat.

During a volcanic eruption, hot liquid magma thrusts itself upward to the surface of Earth through the **parent rock**. The parent rock is the original rock from which other types of rocks are formed. The heat from magma bakes the parent rock and causes new minerals to form.

ROCK FACT

✳ Rocks formed by contact metamorphism, such as marble and slate, are often fine-grained.

▼ *Marble can come in all different colors.*

▼ *Slate is a fine-grained rock that splits into sheets.*

ROCK FACT

✳ Contact metamorphism usually takes place at shallow depths on Earth. At these shallow depths, there is a big difference in temperature between the magma and the parent rock.

LOCAL AFFAIR

Unlike regional metamorphism, contact metamorphism usually takes place within a narrow area.

Contact aureole is the area around a batholith where rocks change from the heat.

Limestone, further away from the heat, changed to "spotted" rock.

Shale changed to slate.

Limestone changed to marble.

Schist changed to gneiss.

Extremely hot magma of granite batholith

THINGS ARE HEATING UP!

(Have an adult help you with this activity.)

You will need:
- 3 pieces of cookie dough
- hot barbecue grill

Place each piece of cookie dough on a different part of the grill.

Make sure one is close to the heat source of the barbecue, one is a bit further away, and the third is even further.

What happens to the piece of cookie dough that is closest to the heat source?

What happens to the piece of cookie dough that is farther from the heat source?

The same thing happens to rocks in relation to heat sources under the surface of Earth.

COLLIDING CONTINENTS

Earth is made up of different layers. The outermost layer of Earth is called the **crust**. Below the crust is the **mantle**, which is a very thick, dense layer of rock.

BELOW THE CRUST

The mantle is approximately 1,800 miles (2,897 km) thick—much thicker than the crust. The **outer core** is inside the mantle. The temperature of the outer core is very hot, but the **inner core** is even hotter. The temperature of the inner core is about $9,000^0$F ($4,982^0$C).

Outer core

Inner core

Lower mantle

Upper mantle

Thin crust of solid rock

WORLD IN MOTION

✳ The continents are always moving. Each year, North America and Europe move approximately one inch (2.5 cm) apart.

DRIFTING CONTINENTS

Earth's crust is divided into giant slabs of moving rock called **tectonic plates**. The Earth's continents are carried on these plates. Approximately 50 million years ago, these moving tectonic plates caused the continents of Asia and India to collide into one another. The Himalayas, the highest mountain range on Earth, formed as a result of the collision.

WHEN PUSH COMES TO SHOVE

You will need:
- modeling clay
- wax paper

Roll out the modeling clay into two sheets.

Place the sheets of clay on the wax paper and push one against the other.

Do you notice how the modeling clay folds and rises at the spots that were pushed together?

The same thing happens when two continents collide. The plates push upward to form mountains.

▼ The boundaries of Earth's major tectonic plates

THE REGIONAL APPROACH

When continents collide they cause great amounts of pressure and heat deep inside Earth, which creates metamorphic rock. Some rocks are metamorphosed over thousands of square miles. This is regional metamorphism.

HEAT AND PRESSURE

Regional metamorphism is caused by intense heat from below the deepest level of solid rock. It is also caused by the immense pressure from layers of overlaying rock, and pressure from movement in Earth's crust. Spectacular mountain ranges, including the Alps and the Andes, were formed when tectonic plates collided and forced rocks upward.

▶ Landscapes may contain marble cliffs.

SMASH IT UP!

You will need:
- three clay balls of different colors
- a plastic knife

Roll the balls together into one big multicolored ball.

Now smash the ball flat.

Stand the flattened ball on its edge and smash it flat again.

With the plastic knife, cut the ball into four pieces and look at the edges.

Notice how the pressure you placed on the clay has made the colors stick together.

In the same way, minerals in metamorphic rocks stick together after being subjected to heat and pressure deep inside Earth.

CREATING MYLONITE

As a vast area of rock grinds past another rock, the tremendous pressure at the points of contact crushes the rock at the meeting points. This action creates a fine-grained metamorphic rock called mylonite. The structure is different from the parent rock, but the minerals in the mylonite still contain the same chemicals.

▲ *The geologist Charles Lapworth introduced the term "mylonite" in 1885.*

MYLONITE TYPES

❋ There are different types of mylonite. Primary mylonite forms during just one metamorphic episode. Secondary mylonite is a mylonite that forms during multiple metamorphic episodes.

MAKING THE GRADE

There are three main types of regional metamorphism, known as **grades**. A grade describes the temperature and pressure conditions under which metamorphic rocks form. The three grades are low, medium, and high. Each grade forms different types of rock.

▲Slate forms during a low-grade metamorphic process.

LOW

Low-grade metamorphism occurs at low pressure and low temperature. Low-grade metamorphic rocks have a lot of minerals that contain water in their crystals. Slate is a low-grade metamorphic rock that forms when relatively low pressure and temperature are applied to clay or shale, which are sedimentary rocks.

▲ Schist is an example of a medium-grade metamorphic rock.

MEDIUM

Medium-grade metamorphism takes place at slightly higher temperatures and higher pressures. Schist is a medium-grade metamorphic rock that forms from more pressure and higher temperatures.

▶ Gneiss is a high-grade metamorphic rock.

UNDER PRESSURE

You will need:

- 24 pea-sized balls of clay in 3 or more different colors
- 5–10 hardcover books
- wax paper

Place the clay balls close together on a piece of waxed paper.

Place a second sheet of waxed paper on top of the clay balls.

Stack the books on top of the waxed paper, spreading the books' weight evenly on the balls underneath.

Remove the books and peel away the waxed paper.

Look at the clay.

Imagine that the books are layers of rock and the clay balls are different colored rocks.

The pressure on the clay balls increases as you add each book.

An entirely new block of clay has been formed within the layers of wax paper.

The same thing happens to metamorphic rocks.

HIGH

High-grade metamorphism takes place at temperatures higher than 600^0F (316^0C) and relatively high pressure. High-grade metamorphic rocks have minerals that contain little water in their crystals. This great increase in pressure and temperature changes schist into gneiss—a hard, glittering rock—forming entirely new crystals.

▼ *535-million-year-old gneiss formations in Chimney Rock State Park, North Carolina*

GNEISS (NICE) DEPOSITS

✳ Gneiss is found all over the world. There are large deposits in the northeastern United States, eastern Canada, Greenland, northern Europe, and Russia.

FOLDING IT UP

Some metamorphic rocks are foliated. This means that they look layered or banded. Gneiss, schist, phyllite, and slate are examples of foliated metamorphic rocks. These rocks may have flat or wavy textural features, which are caused by minerals such as mica. Non-foliated metamorphic rocks, including marble and quartzite, do not have a layered or banded appearance.

▲ Metamorphic rock often has dark wavy lines called foliation.

MINERALS ALIGN

As metamorphic rocks change, the layers of sediment can be folded or become more obvious as pressure on the rock increases. Certain minerals in the rock may become **aligned** in the same direction. For example, when shale turns into slate, it becomes easier to split the well-aligned layers into thin, flat sheets. For this reason, slate is a useful material for roofs and flagstones.

▶ Slate is mostly flaky, gray-colored stone.

PENCILS

Graphite is a mineral only found in metamorphic rocks. The part of a pencil you write with is made of graphite.

▶ *Because it was used in pencils, graphite was named for the Greek word "graphein," which means to draw or write.*

▼ *These rock layers were formed by "folding," which are plate movements not strong enough to change the composition of rocks.*

A GOOD SPLIT

✳ Biotite, chlorite, and quartz are some of the minerals found in slate. Slate splits easily into thin sheets.

▼ *Muscovite is another mineral found in slate.*

FROM LIMESTONE TO MARBLE

Limestone is a sedimentary rock made up mainly of calcite, which is a mineral form of calcium carbonate. Most lakes, rivers, and oceans contain dissolved calcium carbonate. When water **evaporates**, calcium carbonate is left behind, and it may settle on the bottoms of these bodies of water. Calcium-rich mud may eventually form limestone.

▶ *Red and white limestone cliffs at Hunstanton Beach, Norfolk, England*

MARBLE HUNT!

Find something made of marble in your home, school, or community. This could be a floor, countertop, or bathroom fixture.

Look carefully at the marble and notice all the swirls and veins of color it contains.

You now know that these characteristics are caused by other things in the original limestone, such as clay.

GLEAMING STONE

▲ *Carrara marble quarry in Italy*

MARVELOUS MARBLE

Limestone re-crystallizes and turns into marble. Heat and pressure cause the calcite to melt. Marble is a non-foliated rock formed by both regional and contact metamorphism.

Marble can be different colors. It can be pure white, or a mixture of red, green, or brown streaks and patches.

Marble is found in countries all over the world, including Canada, Italy, Germany, and Spain. People dig marble out of **quarries**.

▲ *Green colored marble often comes from India.*

SWIRLY STUFF

Pure limestone forms white marble, but some marble contains swirls and veins of color. If limestone contains clay, it will form reddish-colored marble. If limestone contains serpentine, it will form greenish marble. Other substances in limestone create yellow, black, and purple marble.

▶ *Red marble has been valued for its natural beauty and elegance since the dawn of civilization.*

FOR ALL THE MARBLES!

People use marble to make many things, including buildings, tombstones, fireplace mantles, floor tiles, and countertops, because it is easy to cut and polish. Sculptors use marble to make statues because marble is soft and easy to carve or cut into shapes.

CARRARA MARBLE

One of the most famous types of marble comes from a city in Italy called Carrara. Sculptors have been using this white or blue-gray marble for hundreds of years. The **Pantheon** and **Trajan's Column** are both built out of Carrara marble. Michelangelo, the famous Italian artist, carved his well-known statue *David* out of Carrara marble.

▶ *The original sculpture of David was moved to the Accademia Gallery in Florence, where it attracts many visitors.*

MARBLE SCULPTURE

✳ In 1919, Daniel Chester French completed a huge marble sculpture of Abraham Lincoln, the American president from 1861 to 1865. This sculpture can be seen in the Lincoln Memorial in Washington, DC.

▶ *Marble sculpture of Abraham Lincoln*

MARBLE TOMB

The Indian **emperor** Shah Jahan (1592–1666) constructed the Taj Mahal out of white marble. He built the Taj Mahal as a **tomb** for his favorite wife. It took more than 20 years to complete.

▶ *In 1983, the Taj Mahal became a UNESCO World Heritage Site.*

CALCIUM CARBONATE

Marble contains a chemical called calcium carbonate, which is used in many different **industries**. It is found in paper, toothpaste, plastics, and paints. Approximately three-quarters of the world's ground calcium carbonate comes from marble.

▼ *Toothpaste contains ground marble.*

SHALE INTO SLATE

Shale is a fine-grained sedimentary rock made up of mainly compressed mud. The mud is a mix of clay minerals and microscopic **particles** of other minerals including quartz and calcite. Shale is typically gray in color and tends to break into thin layers.

GOING DEEP

✳ Shale is deposited in water that moves very slowly, including lakes, lagoons, river deltas, and floodplains. It is very common in deep ocean environments.

▼ *Shale cliffs in western Ireland*

SHALE

Shale that is subject to heat and relatively low pressure changes into the metamorphic rock called slate.

KEEPING IT TOGETHER

✳ Mudstone is another clay rock. It is similar to shale, but it does not break into distinct layers as shale does.

▶ *Blue mudstone carved by the sea*

SLATE AHEAD!

Slate is a contact metamorphic rock. It is often found in European countries such as France, Scotland, and Wales, and in the northeastern United States. It is often gray or black in color, but purple, green, or cyan slate also appears in certain parts of the world.

▲ *Slate is a low-grade contact metamorphic rock.*

▼ *Quartz is a mineral that can be found in clay.*

▼ *Calcite crystals come in more than 300 different shapes.*

SLATE IS GREAT!

People use slate for many things including patios, walkways, tabletops, roofs and roof shingles, tiles for floors, and gravestones. It is a particularly good roofing material because it is durable, environmentally friendly, absorbs very little water, and is resistant to frost and freezing.

RAISING THE ROOF

Slate's smooth-surfaced layers make it the perfect material for roofs. It can be split into thin sheets called roofing shingles. The sheets are flat and easy to work with.

▼ *Many houses in England have slate roofs.*

GREAT SLATE

✳ During the 18th and 19th centuries, blackboards in schools were made out of black slate.

▼ *Instead of paper, students used small handheld blackboards called slates, which often had grids to help them keep straight lines.*

OLD SPANISH ROCKS

The region of Galicia in Spain produces 90 percent of the slate that is used for roofing in Europe. This area produces approximately 4 million tons (3.6 million metric tons) of slate per year and some of it's slate deposits are more than 500 million years old.

▲ The slate-producing region of Galicia in northwestern Spain

DIFFERENT COLORS

Purple and green slate comes from Wales, and green slate comes from a county in England called Cumbria.

The slate found in Monson, Maine, is often dark purple or black in color. Various colors of slate are also found in China.

◄ Slate is often mined in huge quarries.

▼ Slate floor tiles are very popular because they come in many colors.

GRANITE INTO GNEISS

Granite is one of the most common rocks on Earth. It is a coarse-grained igneous rock that is made up mainly of the minerals feldspar and quartz. There are also smaller amounts of darker colored minerals, such as biotite and hornblende, in granite. People use granite as a building stone because it is extremely hard and durable.

▼ El Capitan in Yosemite National Park, in California, is almost entirely formed of granite.

▶ Waterfalls in Norway's gneiss regions attract many visitors.

SPARKLING ROCK

Granite that is subject to intense heat and pressure changes into the metamorphic rock called gneiss (pronounced "nice"). Gneiss is a regional metamorphic rock. The name "gneiss" comes from an Old German word that means "sparks." Small bits of minerals, such as quartz and biotite, sparkle and glitter in the rock.

MINERALS IN GNEISS

The mineral prehnite is found in gneiss. Prehnite is often green, but it may be gray, yellowish, or white. Biotite is also found in gneiss. It is one of the most common and important rock-forming minerals. It forms black, brown, or dark green crystals in gneiss.

▼ Biotite is a mineral that can be found in gneiss.

▼ Prehnite does not form distinct crystals like other minerals do.

PARAGNEISS

✳ Gneiss derived from sedimentary rocks, such as sandstone, is called paragneiss.

SOME "GNEISS" USES

For thousands of years, slabs of granite and gneiss have been quarried and used to construct huge buildings and other structures. Like many metamorphic rocks, gneiss often has layers and streaks of dark- and light-colored rock.

MEMORIES

✳ Gneiss slabs are often used for gravestones and memorials. Gneiss is a hard stone and requires skill to carve by hand. Modern methods of carving include using computer-controlled rotary bits and sandblasting.

▼ *Washington Hall and many of the buildings and retaining walls at the U.S. Military Academy in West Point, New York, are made of gneiss.*

USEFUL AND GNEISS

Gneiss is similar to granite, but often has parallel layers. That is why the rock splits easily into straight slabs. This makes it very useful for building walls and paving streets. Gneiss is often called stratified granite.

◄ *Cobblestones are often cut out of gneiss.*

SLEEK SURFACE

Many public and commercial buildings have flooring made of gneiss tiles. Some people have polished granite countertops and floor tiles in their homes. Many so-called granite countertops are actually gneiss. The streaks of dark- and light-colored rock in gneiss make beautiful twirls and patterns in polished countertops.

ANCIENT STATUES

✳ Ancient Egyptians used many different kinds of stones. Gneiss was quarried in the Sahara desert. It was used to make statues and ritual objects.

▶ *This majestic statue of Khafre was carved out of diorite-gneiss. Khafre was a king in ancient Egypt and builder of the second pyramid at Giza.*

27

THE HUMAN TOUCH

People have been digging for and studying metamorphic rocks for hundreds of years. Geologists are scientists who study the history of Earth and its life as recorded in rocks.

FORGET ABOUT FOSSILS

Unlike other types of rock, it is hard to find traces of animals and plants in metamorphic rocks. That is because the high temperatures and pressure that create metamorphic rocks also erase any **fossils**.

▼ *Metamorphic rocks do not usually contain any fossils.*

UNDER PRESSURE

You will need:

- a lump of clay about the size of the palm of your hand.

Take the clay in one hand, and with your other hand, leave fingerprints all over the lump of clay.

Now, roll out the clay several times into a smooth sheet.

What happens to the fingerprints?

The fingerprints are like the remains of plants and animals (fossils) left in metamorphic rock.

The pressure you applied to the clay removed the fingerprints, just like the pressure under the surface of Earth removes the fossils.

CUT AND POLISHED

✳ Gemstones associated with metamorphic rocks are hard mineral crystals that have been cut and polished. Diamonds, emeralds, and rubies are three of the most valued gemstones on Earth.

▼ *Gemstones are cut and polished to be used as jewelry.*

▼ *Abandoned rock quarries can be turned into parks, fishing ponds, and geology classrooms.*

QUESTIONS ABOUT QUARRIES

Quarrying is a form of mining. People mine for large deposits of useful minerals or rocks in quarries. People must dig very deep mines when a useful mineral or rock is found deep below the surface. The mines are dug deeper and deeper until all of the resources are used up. People then use these quarries as **landfill** sites for garbage and other waste. Landfills cause pollution and can harm the habitats of plants and animals.

▼ *Old quarries turned into landfills can pose a danger to wild animals.*

GLOSSARY

aligned Describing something that is in line with something else

batholith Igneous rock that has hardened into an enormous mass deep underground

crust Outermost solid layer of Earth or another planet

curling stones Thick stone disks used in the sport of curling

emperor The ruler of an empire

evaporates Passed off into vapor from a liquid state

foliated A rock that has a layered structure

fossils Traces of organisms preserved in rock

geologists Scientists who study the history of Earth and its life as recorded in rocks

grades The types of regional metamorphism

industries Businesses that provide a particular product or service

inner core A solid sphere in the middle of a fluid core of a planet, such as Earth

intrusion The point where lava or magma enters a rock

landfill A place where garbage and other waste is buried

lava Melted rock on Earth's surface that comes from a volcano

magma Melted rock within Earth

mantle The layer of Earth between the crust and the core

minerals Useful chemicals that occur naturally in the form of crystals

outer core The liquid outer layer of Earth's core

Pantheon A famous building in Rome, Italy, built for the Roman gods

parent rock The original rock from which something else was formed

particle A very small part

quarries Large, open pits for obtaining rocks and minerals

sediment Material within a liquid that settles to the bottom

shock metamorphism Permanent changes in rocks caused by high-pressure shock waves

tectonic plates Massive slabs of moving rock in Earth's crust

tomb A chamber where dead people's bodies are buried

Trajan's Column A monument in Rome, Italy, built in honor of the emperor Trajan

MORE INFORMATION

FURTHER READING

Marble and Other Metamorphic Rocks.
   Chris Pellant and Helen Pellant. Gareth Stevens Publishing, 2007.

Metamorphic Rock.
   Rebecca Faulkner. Raintree, 2007.

Metamorphic Rocks: Recycled Rock.
   Darlene R. Stille. Compass Point Books, 2008.

Born of Heat and Pressure: Mountains and Metamorphic Rocks.
   Patricia L. Barnes-Svarney. Enslow Pub Inc., 2001.

Metamorphic Rocks (Earth Rocks!).
   Holly Cefrey. PowerKids Press, 2003.

Minerals (Rocks, Minerals, and Resources)
   Adrianna Morganelli. Crabtree Publishing. 2004.

WEBSITES

RocksForKids
www.rocksforkids.com/

Geology for Kids
www.kidsgeo.com/geology-for-kids/

Minerology 4 Kids
www.minsocam.org/MSA/K12/K_12.html

How Rocks Are Formed
www.rocksforkids.com/RFK/howrocks.html

INDEX